IMAGES
of America

BREWER

Joshua Lawrence Chamberlain remains Brewer's most celebrated native son. Born in 1828, he graduated with honors from Bowdoin College in 1855, later joining the faculty. As a battlefield commander, he led a bayonet charge at Gettysburg in 1863 and accepted the Confederate surrender at Appomattox Courthouse in 1865. He served four terms as Maine governor, followed by a long life of business, lecturing, and writing that ended with his death in 1914. This government engraving is exhibited at the Brewer Historical Society.

IMAGES
of America

BREWER

Richard R. Shaw

ARCADIA
PUBLISHING

Published by Arcadia Publishing
Charleston, South Carolina

Library of Congress Catalog Card Number: 2008933051

For all general information contact Arcadia Publishing at:
Telephone 843-853-2070
Fax 843-853-0044
E-mail sales@arcadiapublishing.com
For customer service and orders:
Toll-Free 1-888-313-2665

Visit us on the Internet at www.arcadiapublishing.com

Prolific Brewer photographer John Craig Thayer opened his second studio at 21 North Main Street, pictured in the late 1920s. Assisted by his sons, Wilbur and Raymond, Thayer was known as a fine craftsman and a respected human being. Many of his pictures—donated to the Brewer Historical Society by his daughter, Mildred N. Thayer—appear in this book, which is gratefully dedicated to his memory and in her honor.

CONTENTS

No.Main St., Brewer,Me.

North Main Street near the Wilson Street intersection was a bustling city center in the 1920s. Hardware store owners Hazen and Fred Danforth sold Gulf gasoline for 22¢ per gallon. In this image, motorists may be driving to the old city hall, visible behind the trees at top right, or a worship service at the First Congregational Church, top left. The street remains a thriving thoroughfare as Brewer enters the 21st century. The church still beckons Sunday morning worshippers; the city hall was destroyed by fire in 1937.

For more than half a century, from 5:30 a.m. to 9 p.m., the tiny *Bon Ton* boats ferried passengers from lower Wilson Street in Brewer across the river to downtown Bangor. At first the fare was a penny, later increased to 3¢. When the cost spiraled to a nickel during the final crossings of the *Bon Ton III* in 1939, many cried inflation.

INTRODUCTION

Growing up in Bangor in the 1950s and 1960s, I used to wonder why Brewer was called our twin city, since the two communities seemed to have so little in common. My teachers would answer that not every twin is identical and that some of the finest siblings they had ever known did not look alike.

I am reminded of those innocent exchanges today as I complete this look back at Brewer's more than two centuries of sharing the spotlight with its big brother across the river. Bangor's population of some 32,000 is still far ahead of Brewer's population of 9,200. At times, it seems all we share are 7 miles of riverfront and 3 bridges. Do not, however, be deceived by political and athletic rivalries and other differences; the twin cities' roots run deep and spread wide. One needs the other; I think it has always been that way.

Compiling this book of local history, I was struck by the vision and integrity of the town's citizens and how early in its development they figured out how to set it apart from other communities. Aided by a lower waterfront than Bangor's and clay that extended to the shoreline, they built ships, manufactured bricks, harvested ice, and made paper. That brought a surprising, and largely overlooked, prosperity to that side of the Penobscot River. Like the supermarket jingle, Brewer has always been "hometown proud" because of its relatively small population, but nonetheless enjoyed a healthy school system, good public transportation, and major industry.

The town was named for an ambitious Massachusetts native, Col. John Brewer, who trekked into eastern Maine in September 1770, returning to stay in 1771 to oversee the development of 58 square miles of wilderness. At first, the settlement was named New Worcester, after his home town, and encompassed what later became Orrington, Holden, and Brewer. If there were photography in Brewer's day, then this book would have included his portrait, along with such dramatic early events as the brief but troublesome invasion by the British in 1814 of what is now known as Brewer, set off in 1812 as a separate town. The community, which like Bangor is located at the head of river navigation, received its city charter on February 8, 1889.

In the 20th century, Brewer prospered in other ways. Retirees and working professionals were drawn to the well-designed subdivisions of Parkway North and Parkway South. Major industries, such as the Lemforder Corporation, built in Brewer and employed many skilled workers. The 1984 opening of the Veterans Remembrance Bridge brought with it several miles of Interstate 395 that changed the landscape like so many other projects had done throughout the city's history.

From the mid-19th century onward, the community was well photographed. Having combed through hundreds of pictures in various collections, I have tried to hit the many highs, and the occasional lows, of the town's development. It is tempting to remember only the happy times, such as Fourth of July celebrations, soapbox derby races, and sporting victories. But realistically, every town has its darker moments too; these must not be forgotten. That is why I decided to include images of floods, fires, even the Ku Klux Klan marching in full regalia in 1924.

My friend, the late historian James B. Vickery, wrote this comment in the foreword of his 1976 pictorial history of Brewer: "Perhaps you will prefer history in small amounts." This collection of 218 images makes up many small pieces of one town's history. I know you will agree that it adds up to something of great importance.

—Richard R. Shaw, June 2000

The Brewer Congregational Scouts formed on Oct. 25, 1909, four months before the Boy Scouts of America began. In this photograph, Rev. Warren Morse poses in a black hat in the back row, third from the left. Second from the left is Frederick C. Oliver, an English theology student studying in Bangor. Oliver worked with the youth of Brewer's First Congregational Church and decided to introduce them, and America, to scouting, which began in Great Britain in 1908. The Brewer Congregational Scouts were later renamed Troop No. 1.

One

PENOBSCOT RIVER SHIPYARDS

Ship launchings were grand occasions in the mid-to-late 19th century, when Brewer shipyards dominated the lower Penobscot River. The first vessel built in Brewer was the schooner *Triton*, launched in 1800. Stimulated by a booming lumber economy and the Gold Rush of the 1840s, numerous Brewer shipyards, such as the Cooper and Dunning yards, turned a handsome profit. Tycoons in Bangor, the riverfront of which was lined with sawmills, envied the activity in their "twin city."

Lumber vessels were a familiar sight along the waterfront during Brewer's heyday as a river port. This photograph, taken from the railroad yard in Bangor, shows the Smith Planing Mill, the First Congregational church, and the icehouses on the Brewer side of the river. During the cities' peak years as shipping capitals, sailors were said to have skipped from one shore to the other on the decks of tightly grouped ships without getting their feet wet.

Bangor Harbor c. 1880 was alive with the arrival and departure of ships. Many of the larger vessels carried ice and other provisions around the world. Occasionally, a harbor master would step in to settle a dispute between feuding ship captains, both of whom desired the same berth along the Bangor or Brewer shore.

One of the finest photographs ever taken on the Brewer waterfront shows William McGilvery's shipyard and drydock in 1870. McGilvery built two short marine railways for the purpose of hauling the *Alfred Howe* (left) and *Hope* (right) up from the river for repairs. Daredevil workers are perched aloft on the high mast.

The *Thomas J. Stewart*, shown in c. 1892, was a three-masted barkentine launched at E. and I.K. Stetson's shipyard on November 13, 1890. Six years later, the vessel—named for the shipping agent who also founded the *Bangor Daily News*—sank during a hurricane off Sandy Hook, Connecticut, with 1,400 tons of coal.

A two-masted ship dominates this 1890 view of the McGilvery-Stetson shipyard on South Main Street. The monuments of the Oak Hill Cemetery in the background place this yard in the approximate location of a present-day steel shipyard named Kustom Steel at 195 South Main Street. In the background at the left is the *Thomas J. Stewart* under construction.

Built in 1866 at the Gibbs and Phillips yard, the ship *Phineas P. Pendleton* was destined for the Far East trade. Legend has it that it entered an American port only once in 19 years. Its lower masts were painted black, marking the deaths of three of the captain's children from diphtheria off the Peruvian coast.

This 1,117-ton ship, launched from John T. Tewksbury's shipyard on November 6, 1865, suffered an undeserving end. Considered as fine as any ship built on the Penobscot River, the *Jennie Hight* was lost on its maiden voyage on the Florida reefs, en route from Bangor to New Orleans. This photograph, courtesy of the Bangor Public Library, shows the ship in all its glory during its launching.

B·100 Brewer, Me. 11-22-19 Launching the Horace E. Munroe.

Brewer's most photographed ship launching took place at 10:57 a.m. on Saturday, November 22, 1919. The *Horace E. Munroe*, a four-masted schooner, slid down the ways of the Bangor and Brewer Shipbuilding Company while thousands looked on and cheered from both sides of the river. The *Bangor Daily News* reported that "all the whistles within half a mile were sounded in celebration of the event." The ship launching was "something worth celebrating,"

LAUNCHING OF THE HORACE E. MUNROE.

No one was hurt in the collision with Henry McLaughlin & Company's storehouse. The crowd on the dock ran in all directions when the schooner lunged toward it. The largest craft ever launched from a Brewer shipyard weighed 2,500 tons. Tugs berthed the vessel at the shipyard pier, where it received its sparring and rigging.

14

the newspaper stated, "for it isn't very often that $200,000 worth of vessel slides overboard hereabout." Mrs. Munroe of Lewiston, wife of the ship's namesake, splashed a bottle of Poland Spring water across its bow. But the ship slid away so quickly—before the crew could lower its anchors—that the vessel raced toward the Bangor shore and punched a large hole in a storehouse.

A study in transportation modes is evident in this photograph, taken after the schooner rushed toward the High Head section of the Bangor waterfront. Bumper-to-bumper traffic lined South Main Street for one final look at history in the making. Steel-hulled ships had gained favor during World War I, signaling the decline of wooden shipbuilding in cities such as Brewer. Spectators recalled the 1918 launching of the *Charles D. Stanford*, which resulted in the ship getting stuck, requiring a later launching.

Capt. Samuel H. Barbour's name was synonymous with quality shipbuilding in the late 19th century. Between 1875 and 1895, his Brewer shipyard turned out 24 steamers as well as several schooners. This family portrait shows Barbour, his wife, and seven children, c. 1883. Barbour, who died in Brewer in 1896, was general manager of the Bangor and Bar Harbor Steamboat Company.

The Barbour Boat Yard in the 1890s was a beehive of activity. This photograph shows the steamer *Sedgwick* (right), looming over the smaller vessels while in drydock. The *Sedgwick* and the *Silver Star* were built at the yard in 1886. A church steeple, along with other Bangor landmarks, is visible across the river in the distance, placing the boat yard just south of the present-day Joshua Chamberlain Bridge.

Florence Barbour Thomas studies a display of Barbour family portraits and ships in October 1975. She is pictured as a girl on the facing page in the foreground, sitting between her mother and father. Captain Barbour's excursion boats plied the islands of Penobscot and Frenchman bays. Many of the steamers were sold and operated out of Vinalhaven and connected with Camden, Castine, and other Maine ports.

Summer travelers did not have to be millionaires to feel as such when gliding along on well-built steamers like the *Verona*, built and launched at Sam Barbour's shipyard in 1902. The last of the great Barbour boats carried passengers down the Penobscot River on the Bangor-to-Bar Harbor run and measured 110 feet long, 28 feet wide, drew 8 feet of water, had a gross tonnage of 140, and a top speed of 14 knots. In 1907, the *Verona* was lost to fire in Highland Falls, New York, after being sold to a Connecticut company.

Smaller steam vessels added to the activity on the river. This boat, reputed to be the *Lyndria*, is shown in the middle of the Penobscot River with the densely packed buildings of the Bangor waterfront in the distance. Other colorfully named steamers like the *Nellie Kane*, the *Susie May*, the *Goldenrod*, the *Winona*, and the *Navis*, were all build at Samuel Barbour's yard.

Excursionists enjoy light conversation aboard the steamer *Cimbria*, built at the Barbour yard in 1882. John M. Richardson, in his book *Steamboat Lore of the Penobscot*, writes that the *Cimbria* "was considered the most beautiful and most successful of the Barbour boats." Regarded as the most profitable of the river steamers, the *Cimbria* was named for a Russian troop ship that ran aground off Southwest Harbor in 1878.

The Oakes shipyard was located at the foot of Wilson Street, the later location of the Barbour yard. The three steamers identified are the *Nellie Kane*, the *Little Buttercup*, and the *Queen City*, which ran most of its days to Bar Harbor. The *Queen City* was actually built by Samuel Barbour, not Oakes.

Although this photograph from the James Vickery collection at the Bangor Public Library is undated and unidentified, it nonetheless tells its own story. The two-masted vessel is tied up at a wharf along South Main Street, with the steeple of the First Congregational church, a mill smokestack, and piles of lumber visible in the background. No doubt the vessel was waiting to be loaded with lumber.

Two

EDUCATING THE
GENERATIONS

Brewer prides itself on a healthy blend of academics and athletics. This 1920s, 13-member Brewer track team, pictured with its managers and faculty advisor, appears intent on licking the competition. The variety of footwear is remarkable compared to today's sleek running shoes.

The first baseball team organized at the Page Grammar School on Center Street is shown in this 1913 postcard view. Students in the rambling wooden building ranged from kindergarten to sixth grade. The size and maturity of these team members, who competed with other Brewer grammar schools, suggests they were enrolled in Page's top grade. Teacher George W. Burrill is shown standing in the center of the back row.

This handsome brick edifice overlooking the river now provides apartments for the elderly, managed by the Brewer Housing Authority. Many may remember when it was the Dirigo Grammar School, constructed in 1910–1911. Longtime Brewer resident Paul E. Tower recalls transferring to Dirigo after the Page Grammar School burned in 1941. Resentful Dirigo students derided the new arrivals as "Page School bums" Eventually, however, they learned to share their classroom space.

March 22, 1941, was a day of infamy for Brewer after the Page Grammar School was destroyed by a blaze that lasted five hours. Fire chief Irving Doyle said an overheated furnace pipe started the inferno. Ken Ward, then a high school freshman living on nearby Parker Street, later wrote that the strange musical sounds he heard that Saturday resulted from teacher Mildred Thayer's piano crashing into the basement from her second-floor classroom.

Page School students, probably first grade, are pictured in the school's happier days in a 1912 class portrait. When the school burned in 1941, principal Margaret Hatfield Danforth commented that the building "wasn't just a school. Page School was the most competitive school in the Brewer school system and proved it each year when intramural field days were held. It set records and fiercely defended them each year."

Admired by students and educators alike, veteran teacher Mildred N. Thayer left her mark on the Brewer school system. She may be best remembered for the years she taught at the Page Grammar School, where she comforted students during and after a devastating fire. Thayer retired from the Bangor school system in 1971, having taught science at Garland Street Junior High School since 1951.

The South Brewer Grammar School was similar in design to the Page School, also enrolling students in kindergarten through sixth grade. Built in 1906, it was abandoned in the 1970s, but later purchased by the Epstein family as a clothing store annex. In recent years, the building has housed the Epstein antiques emporium. Parochial students attended St. Teresa's School, also located in South Brewer.

Class portrait day was always a thrilling event at this school in South Brewer. The young students, some shown sitting, would step out into the morning sunshine and smile for the photographer. The removal of the large wooden building, which boasted a bell tower that was visible for some distance, eventually made way for modern development.

Another grammar school, the Sargent School, was located at South Main and Pendleton Streets. These schools were officially two-story in design. In the days before stringent fire codes, however, they likely totaled four stories, with attic and cellar space factored in. The front part of the building having been removed, the former schoolhouse is now the home of Van Raymond Outfitters at 388 South Main Street.

This roomy, well-lit study hall stands in stark contrast to the cramped quarters of Brewer's earlier schools. Two students are shown studying in one of 24 classrooms of the modern high school on Parkway South. This newspaper photograph was published on September 30, 1958, soon after the school's opening. Its caption stressed the rooms' "restful colors and modern fixtures" and the "pleasure of hours spent at study."

The new elementary school on Washington Street was nearing completion when this picture was taken in January 1952. First classes in the $240,000 building were held the following September, and dedication and open house programs were conducted in the early fall. The school originally contained 11 multipurpose rooms and remains one of the city's busiest and most popular centers of learning.

State Street School was completed in 1948 and designed to accommodate a normal enrollment of 250. Architect Alonzo J. Harriman and general contractor T.W. Cunningham added the semicircular glass wing for a kindergarten classroom, including its own entrance and exit. The enrollment had ballooned to more than 400 by the late 1950s, when graphic artist Tom Kane included this sketch of what was then a grade school for kindergarten through seventh grade in his portfolio of local landmarks.

Lee V. Hallowell learned every aspect of Brewer education from 1959 to 1975, when he served as superintendent of schools. His professional but gentle demeanor won him many friends in Brewer and in other places, including Bangor, where he was principal of the Hannibal Hamlin and Fifth Street Junior High Schools. Hallowell was educated at Machias Normal School, Boston University, and the University of Maine, where he received a master's degree in education.

Brewer's first free public high school was opened in 1873, with classes held in the town hall, and later in the Brimmer Street School. In this June 10, 1889 photograph, students and faculty pose in front of the new high school building at South Main and School Streets. Long after the school was closed for general study, manual training students returned to this building for instruction. A modern elementary school was later constructed in its place.

Frank A. Floyd changed the face of Brewer education when he organized the so-called classical high school in the fall of 1873. The free school's first principal, Floyd was a Bowdoin graduate sent to Brewer with the highest recommendation of college president Joshua L. Chamberlain. Floyd's 1940 obituary lauded the 92-year-old as a respected educator, banker, and attorney, having been admitted to the Penobscot County Bar in 1876.

It is no wonder that the young man in the front row is smiling, as he is surrounded by 12 young women, comprising the entire Brewer High School graduating class of 1911. The class, shown sitting on the front steps of the old high school on South Main Street, enjoyed a rare graduation trip to Washington, D.C., in lieu of traditional commencement exercises.

The brick Brewer High School on Somerset Street was opened for the fall term on September 13, 1926. The old school was small and showing its age, so in 1921 the city council and the new Parent-Teacher Association set out to build a new school. Although originally planned for South Main and School Streets, the building was eventually sited a short distance away. It later became a junior high school and finally an enlarged and modernized three-year middle school.

An enrollment of 488 students in grades 10 through 12 entered the latest Brewer High School for its fall opening in 1958. The school is located on land containing more than 20 acres. A new building for industrial arts was added in 1968, and an annex was added two years later. Students spanning the traditional four years now attend the school.

When Lura Hoit began working at Brewer High School as the girls' physical education instructor in 1940, the only sport offered to females was basketball. Highlights of her 28-year career included taking over for the boys' physical education teacher, being a World War II draftee, and receiving an honor award from the Maine Association for Physical Education and Recreation on her retirement in 1968.

The Se Beowulf Club was founded in 1933 by Marjorie Marsh and Natalie Bridgham to stimulate interest in English, and later to encompass public service, leadership, and character development. Fifteen Brewer High School sophomore girls were eligible for yearly membership. Those posing on the club's 40th anniversary in 1973 for a yearbook portrait, from left to right, are as follows: (front row) Marjorie Marsh Quigg; Marjorie Jenkins, advisor; and Gloria Blier, secretary; (back row) Patrice Tremble, vice president; Lisa Williams, treasurer; and Kathy Higgins, president.

SCHOOL SONG

STAND UP AND CHEER FOR BREWER
CHEER FOR A BREWER VICTORY
CHEER FOR THE GOOD OLD WITCHES
THE ORANGE AND THE BLACK FOR ME.
CHEER FOR OUR ALMA-MATER
WE'RE TELLING YOU SHE IS SWELL
FIGHT, FIGHT, FIGHT FOR BREWER
THE SCHOOL WE ALL LOVE SO WELL!

— HEYWOOD S. JONES

Brewer High School's cheering song had an unusual beginning. Composer Heywood S. Jones was slowed in traffic after attending a Veterans Day football contest between Bangor and Brewer when the words and music came into his head. He wrote the song later that evening. On November 22, 1940, a male quartet led by music instructor Linwood Bowen first performed the number at a school assembly. Jones also penned the cheering songs for Bangor High School and John Bapst High School, a parochial institution.

Six energetic students comprised the high school cheerleading squad in 1930. Clara Swan, front row center, went on to earn a doctorate, becoming a highly respected business instructor at Husson College in Bangor. The other students, from left to right, are as follows: (front row) Rene DeMers and Bill Crockett; (back row) Lillian Topham, Dorothy Marsh, and Grace Sargent.

32

Three

BREWER MEANS BUSINESS

Dana Witman and Loren Thompson pose in front of the Thompson Print shop, then located on lower Wilson Street. One of Brewer's more durable businesses traces its roots to 1904, when Thompson started operations in a converted chicken coop just above the railroad tracks on Wilson Street, soon moving to the location mentioned above and later to the corner of South Main and Wilson Streets. The proximity to the *Bon Ton* ferry dock worked to Thompson's advantage, as he made deliveries to Bangor on the tiny boat. Today the business is operated by Tom Smith, formerly owned by his father, Ken Smith.

Forrest B. Marsh's grocery store was a fixture at the corner of North Main and Wilson Streets early in the 20th century. He operated the business with Hazen and Fred Danforth. For years, the scales in front of the store were the only weighing mechanism in Bangor and Brewer. Recalled Marsh's daughter, Marjorie Marsh Quigg, in 1993, "Dad could grab a barrel [of flour] and put it on his shoulder, and go right up the stairs to an apartment on the second floor."

F. Herbert Hathorn manufactured boot calks and performed machine work in the rear of this rambling brick building at 75 South Main Street. The Hathorn Manufacturing Company was established in 1893; by the 1920s, Bert Hathorn was tooling around Brewer in this White steamer, which he used for the purposes of both business and pleasure. Many refer to the brick block as the old box factory since the Bangor Box Company occupied the front section.

A later view of the Union block at North Main and Wilson Streets shows a name change of Danforth Brothers Hardware. Next-door is an A&P grocery. The little house in the distance at the left was the second photographic studio of J. Craig Thayer. The block is still standing and usually fully occupied, although the name Danforth and A&P have gone the way of the old-fashioned gasoline pumps in the front yard.

Charles O. and Edward P. Farrington opened this general store in 1849, stocked with groceries, dry goods, woolen clothing, and hardware. The sign over their Center Street business boasted that their hardware was "cheaper than in Bangor." Brewer Savings Bank, located upstairs, had moved to North Main Street when Maurice B. MacLaughlin bought the store around 1930; he sold it to Arthur C. Thompson and Lawrence "Bud" Lyford in 1945. Thompson and Lyford hardware was later operated by Lyford's brother-in-law, Bill Hayes, and other family members.

This imposing wooden block at 46 Center Street, known in later years as the address of Landry's Inc. appliances, earlier was Benjamin F. Young's grocery, meat, and fish store. The "Ship Stores" sign around the corner suggests an extension of Young's business, specializing in mariners' provisions. St. Joseph's Catholic Church had a parish hall upstairs. Empire Laundry shared the building, beside which later was J. Craig Thayer's third photographic studio.

T&K stores were noted for their variety of merchandise and helpful clerks. Standing amidst the Rinso soap powder and Sunkist oranges inside the T&K store at 471 South Main Street, c. 1937, are proprietor Otis Verow, left, and his son, Clement. Clement, the father of veteran city clerk Archie Verow, who loaned this picture for publication, later operated a Nationwide store at 523 South Street in the Epstein block.

These two buildings located on the sharp turn on Route 15 in South Brewer were landmarks around the turn of the 20th century. At the left is the post office and store operated by the Southworth Brothers. Sewall B. Southworth was the assistant postmaster as early as 1894. Next door is the Edgar A. Stanley home. Sharp eyes will spot Edgar's mother seated in the front window nearest the door.

James S. Ayer's store at the corner of South Main and Century Streets sold groceries, meats, hardware, shipping supplies, dry goods, boots, shoes, gentlemen's furnishings, wallpaper, oil cloth, and straw matting. A 1914 advertisement features Ayer's motto, "Headquarters for low prices."

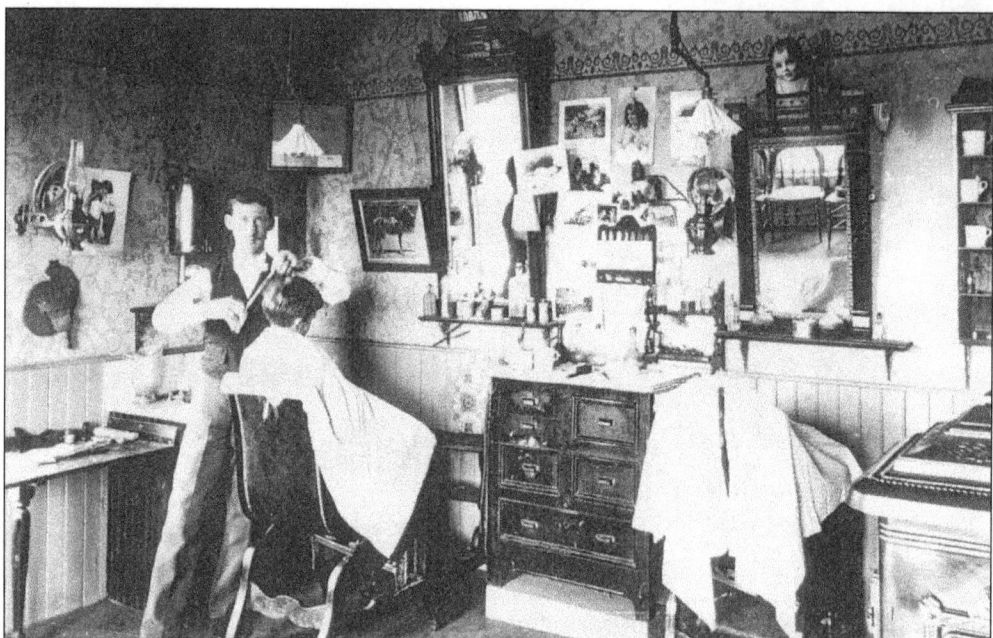

The kerosene lantern, ornate wallpaper, and well-dressed barber date this picture, courtesy of the Brewer Public Library, from the distant past, not the present. Art Rogers is shown giving a 15¢ haircut to Percy Sargent inside a second-story barbershop located in South Brewer. Sewell S. Herrick operated a grocery on the ground floor.

The barbershop's wallpaper might well have been purchased at Henry B. Washburn's paint store at Center and North Main Streets. The store's upper sign states Washburn is a "practical painter." In 1888, he advertised a full line of paints, oils, varnish, wallpaper, and borders. He also provided a decorating service for churches and public halls and private residences.

The Brewer Savings Bank was founded in May 1869 with William P. Burr as president and Edward P. Farrington as treasurer. Frank Floyd and his sons, Henry and Howard, as well as Wyman Gerry were later presidents. This three-story brick block on North Main Street was the bank's home for many years.

A 1949 newspaper advertisement heralded the grand opening of the new, enlarged Ferris Store at Parker and North Main Streets. Assisted by his wife Selma and later by his son Joseph and his daughter Gayle, Elias Ferris sold "wares for all the family since 1926." Competition from Zayre and other large retailers put Elias, the son of an immigrant Lebanese mother, out of business in 1968.

Grand Opening

TODAY -- Of the NEW
FERRIS STORE

165 North Main St.,   **Brewer, Me.**

A New and Larger Store With Many New Departments
Two and One-half Floors of Merchandise.

COME AND SEE OUR
MANY SPECIALS!
BARGAINS GALORE!
NEW MERCHANDISE!
NEW LOW PRICES!

FREE GIFTS TO ALL

MEN'S DEPARTMENT	INFANT'S DEPARTMENT
WORK CLOTHES	SWEATERS
UNDERSHIRTS	OVERALLS
DRESS SHIRTS	JACKETS
JACKETS	BLANKETS
SWEATERS	DIAPERS
BRIEFS	PANTS
SHORTS	SHIRTS
HOSE	SLIPS

Ladies' Apparel
SWEATERS
SLIPS
SKIRTS
PANTIES
BRAS
NIGHTGOWNS
PAJAMAS
HOSIERY
APRONS
SOX
HANDBAGS
DRESSES

Children's Back To School Needs

PANTIES	PANTS
DRESSES	SWEATERS
SLIPS	JACKETS
SHIRTS	SOX

SCHOOL SUPPLIES
PENCILS, PENCIL BOXES, INK, RULERS, NOTEBOOKS, PAPER
GLUE, INDEX TABS

FINEST UNDER THE SUN
Footman-Hillman
DAIRIES INC.
DAIRY PRODUCTS
DIAL 4527
VISITORS ALWAYS WELCOME

Golden Guernsey Milk   Cottage Cheese

Homogenized Milk   Cultured Buttermilk

Chocolate Milk   Country Fresh Eggs

Footman Hillman

149 STATE STREET   TEL. 4527   BREWER, MAINE

The friendly milkman from Footman-Hillman Dairies, formerly Footman Dairy, is a relic from the past. The dairy was founded in September 1920 by Glen H. Footman. It started with a milk delivery of 200 quarts, delivered by horse and wagon, and increased to a major business, dealing in all dairy products and employing more than 50 people by its 50th anniversary in 1970.

J. Albert Cowan—pictured on the left in February 1935 along with a friend, Henry Jordan—began pumping gasoline and servicing automobiles in 1933. In 1946, Cowan's Amoco station moved from 149 South Main Street across the street to its present location, 146 South Main Street. Albert's son, James, joined the business in 1950, followed by James' son, Phillip, in 1974.

Henry "Cap" Morrill stares somberly into the camera at his South Main Street bar during World War II. The three stars on the flag behind him signify that his three sons—Henry B., James, and Carleton—are off in Europe fighting the Nazis. The youngest of the four sons, Richard, would soon join his brothers in the army. Cap retired after the war ended and his four sons took over the family business.

Artist Wally McQuarrie was up to the challenge of repainting the exterior of the Cap Morrill's Fish Market in South Brewer. What better representation is there of Maine and fishing than a depiction of the red and white striped lighthouse at West Quoddy Head, surrounded by fishing boats, traps, and lobsters? Today, the wholesale fish market is operated by Cap's grandson Phil Morrill in a modern building in an industrial park. The South Main Street property with the painting outside is now called the Captain's Market, operated by Frank Breau.

Penobscot Square was a little sadder the day in 1988 when Leslie Maxwell Ohmart Jr. retired from his pharmacy and especially when he died a decade later. Ohmart bought the old Hinkley pharmacy in 1953, building it into a major area business. He also was a friend of youth, known for his promotion of alcohol-free graduation parties.

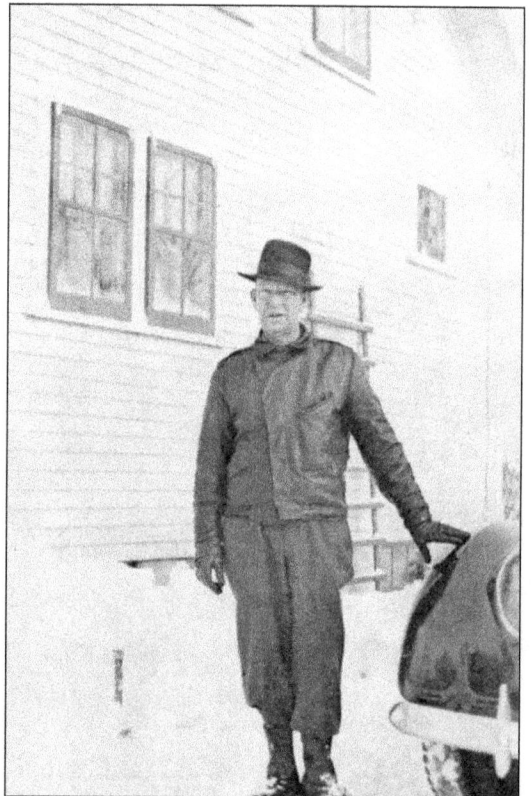

In the 1920s, George Landry Sr. sold ringer washing machines for the Bangor Maytag Company and also started a part-time business in his garage at 159 Chamberlain Street in Brewer. His appliance company blossomed into Landry's Inc., moving to 46 Center Street in 1964. Landry died suddenly in 1947, but his daughter, Ruth, and later her brother, George Jr., took over the business, aided by other family members.

Harold "Harry" Epstein (1904–1988) was a basketball player, musician, and devout member of the Beth Israel Synagogue. But he is best remembered for the South Brewer clothier he operated for 66 years. Epstein's, founded in 1910 by Harry's father Max, sold work clothes and boots to mill workers. Harry was assisted by his wife, Ruth, his daughter, Eleanor, and his son-in-law, Stanley Israel.

CHARLES L. DRILLEN

Charles L. Drillen, Founder Of Spring Water Farm, Dies

The 1956 obituary of Charles Drillen, founder of the Oak Grove Spring Water Company in North Brewer, states that his spring water farm had served thousands of Bangor and Brewer residents since its founding nearly 50 years before. Discovered by the Farrington family in the mid-1800s, the spring was favored by ship captains. The company made its last delivery by horse and wagon around 1945 and continues to be operated by the Drillen family.

W.H. Shurtlett & Company of Portland opened this wholesale distributing plant in 1956. The dealer in salt, chemicals, and poultry supplies bought about 10 acres at 162 Parkway South and constructed a new warehouse and office building, later expanding its business. The company was kept busy selling rock salt during the ice storm of January 1998, when roads and rooftops were coated with layers of devastating ice buildup.

Advertising the world's lowest priced fuel would be out of the question these days, but 60 years ago the Robinson-Kenney company had that slogan painted on its delivery trucks. Harold P. Robinson and Donald C. Kenney sold fuel oil and oil burners at 53 Center Street. This photograph shows a company truck refueling the coast guard cutter USS *Algonguin* at High Head in Bangor on March 28, 1939. It took two and a half hours to fill the icebreaker.

Four

TO BANGOR
AND BEYOND

This early postcard view shows the toll and railroad bridges not long after the turn of the 20th century. The passenger bridge was built in 1846, following a spring flood that destroyed a virtually identical covered bridge in the same location. This bridge, in turn, was damaged in a 1902 flood. Tolls on the second bridge are said to have paid for the bridge many times over. Before the Joshua Chamberlain Bridge opened downstream in the 1950s, this bridge was the only solid link between Bangor and Brewer.

The three consecutive boats known as the *Bon Ton I*, *Bon Ton II*, and *Bon Ton III* provided a link to Bangor before a second bridge was built connecting lower Wilson Street in Brewer with Union Street and downtown Bangor. Although the third ferry ceased operation after a fire in 1939, its legacy lives on even among the generations who were born long after its demise.

The *Bon Ton II* was built in 1911 and ran until 1922, when the *Bon Ton III* took over. Historian Mildred N. Thayer writes, "The small steamboat ran daily from 5:30 to 9:00. We are told that after 9 o'clock at night a rowboat ferry was available for those latecomers who still desired ferry service. For many years Mr. Edwin Lora, a Civil War veteran, ran the late rowboat ferry."

Capt. George Jacobs was only one of the colorful characters who piloted the boat back and forth, starting service in 1912. Jacobs recalled, "At a penny a person, one can imagine the ferry trips it had to make to earn $500." He said that his pay was $15 for an 87-hour week, but that this pay was supplemented by Saturday night bonus pay. The ferry ran two extra hours that night; Capt. Jacobs split the bonus with two other crew members and the owner. This bonus amounted to $1.75 apiece.

This rare view shows one of the *Bon Ton* ferries leaving the Brewer ferry slip, with Brewer, not Bangor, in the background. The vessel, which Robert Ripley listed as the smallest steam-driven boat in America, made its last run on November 9, 1939. About an hour after docking for the night, the boat burst into flames and was destroyed. The fire was believed to have been started by the coal furnace, which was banked each night for the next morning's run. The fire marked the end of an era in intercity transportation.

This panoramic view of the old covered toll bridge is a study in contrasting modes of transportation. In the foreground are the tracks of Maine Central Railroad yard in Bangor. Freights and passenger trains left daily on an iron bridge parallel to the wooden one (its granite abutments are barely visible beneath the wooden structure). Moored in the river is a six-masted schooner, and no doubt inside the bridge are horses and wagons traveling between the twin cities. Pedestrians also used the link, although not so many after dark. It is an odd commentary

on the interesting relationship between Bangor and Brewer that the Bangor entrance was an ornate portal facing into the 440-foot span, while Brewer's entrance was more austere, usually adorned with an advertisement over the top. As early as 1812, when Brewer split from Orrington, settlers were intrigued with the thought of linking to its sister across the river. The first bridge built across the Penobscot River became a reality in 1846. In later years, trolley tracks were laid on the second bridge to connect with Bangor.

The rambling wooden Burr Block on the left greeted visitors to State Street. This photograph, taken after the all-steel bridge was opened to traffic in 1912, shows the Brewer railroad switching house at right and gasoline pumps at the far right. A covered railroad bridge—built for the Bangor & Bucksport Railroad and later replaced by a steel structure—was opened in 1873. It later shared the tracks with Maine Central Railroad trains.

An earlier photograph taken from a somewhat different angle shows the twin covered bridges and an old railroad crossing sign at the far right. There were no flashing lights and automatic gates back then. Note the twin entrances for passengers on either side of the passenger bridge—quite a luxury, as covered bridges normally only had one or none at all. Sometimes youngsters ran afoul of the law by daring each other to walk across the railroad bridge both when it was covered and after the open steel bridge was opened.

James J. Coulter rented out horse-drawn buckboards (rough, open wagons) and hacks (finished carriages) at his livery and boarding stable at the corner of Wilson and South Main Streets. Coulter also provided service for funerals and weddings. Renamed Smart and Bartlett's, the block was consumed by fire on July 4, 1924, reportedly caused by a carelessly tossed firecracker. (A related fire photograph appears on page 113.)

The old iron bridge, as seen from the Bangor railroad yard, always seemed old to many growing up in the twin cities, but there was a time when postcard views, such as this one, showed it off as an engineering achievement. The long span was built by E.E. Greenwood, an engineer from Skowhegan, Maine. It lasted until 1997, when it was declared unsafe and replaced by the four-lane Penobscot Bridge.

Miles of railroad track slice through the city's residential neighborhoods and out into the open countryside. One such route was known locally as the Washington County track since the Bar Harbor Express carried vacationers from Philadelphia, New York, and other points to Maine's easternmost county. Many also traveled to Mount Desert Ferry at Hancock Point, where they boarded steamers for the 8-mile trip across Frenchman Bay to Mount Desert Island.

This open touring car appears ready to roll down the dirt streets of Brewer, and perhaps to other communities, to help its owner deliver a baby or perform a critical operation. Dr. J. Albert Lethiecq (pronounced La-Check) had an office in the darkly colored building at 115 Wilson Street and lived at 178 Wilson Street. Physicians often owned the first automobiles in town. Granite horse hitching posts behind the car offer a study in changing eras.

Brewer's little wooden railroad station between Parker and Wilson Streets could not compare to Bangor's opulent terminal on Washington Street. But the Maine Central Railroad office at Brewer Junction, shown here, eliminated the need for residents to cross over to Bangor simply to ride back over to Brewer en route to points east.

The Bangor Railway & Electric Company operated streetcars such as this, shown c. 1920 near the old high school on South Main Street, to connect with its other lines across the river. The "cow catcher" on the car's front probably scooped up wandering pets. Mildred N. Thayer typed on the back of this photograph, "[Banker] Wyman Gerry [said] one of the young people in the bank doubted . . . that we had trolley cars here. This is proof."

The well-designed Joshua Chamberlain Bridge takes vehicles over the approximate route of the old *Bon Ton* ferries. A toll bridge until 1971 (the toll booth is visible at the far right in Brewer), the span was opened in 1955. Its construction was funded with state and federal money. It was truly a Maine product, from the cement, to the granite, to the stone, and even the labor. Steel, not produced in Maine, was the one product that was imported.

A third bridge linking the twin cities was opened to great fanfare and a parade on Veterans Day 1984. After much discussion about how and where such a span should be built, it was decided to extend the Interstate 395 artery in Bangor across Wilson Street in Brewer. The bridge is much higher than the other two upstream. This aerial view was photographed by Brian Swartz of the *Bangor Daily News*.

54

This aerial photograph taken in October 1954 shows the Joshua Chamberlain Bridge under construction. Ticket takers in the toll booth in the bottom foreground gave motorists little magnetic vinyl pouches in which to insert extra tickets and attach to automobile dashboards. Loren H. Thompson had the distinction of being the first ticket holder when the bridge was opened to traffic in 1955.

More than a dozen people flying a variety of small airplanes flew into the municipal airport on August 25, 1990, after the Brewer Flying Club decided it was time to focus attention on the aging airstrip. Located at the end of Parkway South, the runway is a patchwork of asphalt and dirt. Club president Wanda Leighton said the fly-in generated $533 to improve the field.

ON THE ROAD TO LUCERNE AND BAR HARBOR FROM BANGOR. MAINE

This 1934 postcard view shows a far different Route 1A than the commercial strip of today. The road across Whiting Hill on the stretch of Wilson Street known as the Bar Harbor Road was comparatively narrow then, with only four vehicles visible, all heading toward Brewer. In 1984, the road was widened to four lanes when the Interstate 395 interchange was built.

56

Five

FIRST FAMILIES

Early silhouettes from the collection of the Maine Historic Preservation Commission suggest the dignified bearing of two early settlers, Col. and Mrs. Joshua Chamberlain Sr. The patriarch of the Chamberlain clan left Cambridge, Massachusetts, to settle near the Penobscot River around 1799, later clearing a farm and building a house on North Main Street in Brewer. During the War of 1812, the British destroyed two of the colonel's ships in the river, raising his ire and causing financial hardship.

Portrait artist Norman Rockwell might have been intrigued by the craggy face of Col. Joshua Chamberlain Sr., seen here in his advancing years. The old shipbuilder's struggles were not lost on his grandson, the future Civil War hero Joshua Lawrence Chamberlain, who was a 29-year-old college instructor when his grandfather died in 1857 at age 87. The elder Chamberlain lived the remainder of his years at his farm on North Main Street.

Joshua Chamberlain Jr., the son of the shipbuilder and father of the Civil War commander, was born in Orrington, then part of Brewer, in 1800. He was widely respected for his knowledge of farming, timberlands, and surveying. A strict Calvinist, he was one of the community leaders who oversaw the construction of a Congregational meetinghouse in 1828. Joshua Lawrence Chamberlain's later writings, however, speak not of a household filled with fire and brimstone, but of warmth and love.

When Sarah Dupee Brastow married Joshua Chamberlain Jr., a solid union was forged between the hard-working farmer and the cultured descendant of French Huguenots. Joshua Lawrence Chamberlain was born a little over a year after their 1827 wedding. The daughter of a Revolutionary War soldier and also a deeply religious woman, Sarah was described by biographer Diane Monroe Smith as being responsible for encouraging Lawrence's future life in the ministry.

Many joyous family gatherings as well as times of crisis were spent inside the family home at 80 Chamberlain Street. Young Joshua Lawrence used to study and write in the attic under one of the dormers that faced the river. Brian Higgins, a Chamberlain reenactor and family historian, has identified Lawrence's parents, Joshua Jr. and Sarah, standing in the front yard in this photograph, as well as his sister Sarah, or "Sae," and possibly Lawrence himself.

This was the farm in North Brewer that Col. Joshua Chamberlain built and called home for many years during his marriage to Sarah Dupee Brastow. In 1999, a large framed photograph similar to this was discovered in the Brewer City Hall and donated to the Brewer Historical Society. Contrary to published reports, this was not the birthplace of Joshua Lawrence Chamberlain; that home is pictured on the next page.

A stone tablet correctly identifies this North Main Street house as the true birthplace of Joshua Lawrence Chamberlain; the date of his birth was September 8, 1828. Known as "the cottage" because of its relatively small dimensions, the home was built by Lawrence's father. The elder Chamberlian later built the farm at 80 Chamberlain Street, where the expanding family moved directly from North Main Street.

JOSHUA CHAMBERLAIN
Died Aug 10 1880 Æ 80yrs
SARAH D. BRASTOW
his wife
Died Nov. 5 1888 Æ 83yrs
HORACE B. CHAMBERLAIN

The parents of Joshua Lawrence Chamberlain and one of his three brothers are listed on this tombstone in Brewer's Oak Hill Cemetery. Horace Beriah Chamberlain was born in 1834 and died in 1861 of consumption. Of his death, older brother Lawrence wrote, "One of the greatest sources of pleasure in this world [has been] sealed up."

Born on April 29, 1841, Tom Chamberlain was the youngest of the four Chamberlain brothers. He stood 5 feet, 9 inches, slightly taller than his brother Lawrence, had black hair, weighed only 120 pounds, and was the most athletic of the boys. His parents, who did not want their young son risking his life over slavery, finally relented, and he went off to war in 1862, under the constant protection of Lawrence as he fought by his side in the 20th Maine Regiment. Lieutenant Chamberlain accompanied the regiment at Gettysburg in 1863. At a later battle, he tracked down two battlefield surgeons who saved Lawrence's life.

John Calhoun Chamberlain was a rock of self-assurance, a pacifist who behaved admirably on the battlefield and off. Born on August 1, 1838, John was handsome, good-natured, and humorous like his brother Horace. Like older brother Lawrence, he had a serious side, writes Diana Halderman Loski, "keenly feeling the need to place himself in good employment and to marry well." A graduate of the Bangor Theological Seminary, John was chaplain of the 11th Maine Regiment and later was minister of a church in Castine. He died in 1867.

Chamberlain biographer John J. Pullen referred to the former battlefield commander as "the reluctant Republican" because of the awkwardness as Maine's four-term governor (1867–1870). Joshua Lawrence Chamberlain found the job of governor both rewarding and frustrating. Often, he was unable to parlay his military skills into effective civilian leadership. Never lacking in bold ideas, he had difficulty accomplishing his goals. He was especially bothered by the departure of large numbers of Maine's young citizens to the milder climate and fertile soils of the American West.

This famous military portrait of Chamberlain has served as the basis for a color painting, a sculpture at Brewer's Chamberlain Freedom Park, and even a label for Chamberlain Pale Ale, created by the Shipyard Brewing Company of Portland, Maine. Although he was an ordained minister, the colonel (he was promoted to the rank of general after his gallantry at the Battle of Gettysburg) enjoyed a drink on occasion. Some scholars believe that were he living today, his modesty would discourage his lionization in movies such as *Gettysburg*, based upon the Pulitzer Prize-winning novel *The Killer Angels*.

63

Rev. George W. Field, standing at the center, was pastor of the First Congregational Church when this 19th-century portrait was taken. Seated third from the left is Dr. Horatio N. Page, shown with his family. Field later led the Central Church in Bangor, but returned for the new Brewer church's dedication in 1890, stating that he was glad this "oldest society on the Penobscot was the first to branch out and build as fine as church as they can afford."

The oldest frame house in Brewer has withstood the ravages of time and still stands on State Street. The building replaced an earlier log cabin built by Capt. John Holyoke, whose family later built the brick mansion at the corner of State and North Main Streets pictured on page 65.

John Holyoke's brick house high on the hill at State and North Main Streets was demolished during roadway widening as the Penobscot Bridge was built in 1997. But its legend and mystery live on. Historian Brian Higgins and state representative Richard Campbell, among others, are convinced the residence contained a tunnel stretching 200 yards to the Penobscot River, through which escaping slaves would crawl to the home's safe haven while en route to Canada. Philip and Josephine Christmas later operated a carpet business in the home.

When John Holyoke died in 1885, his last will and testament revealed that he had bequeathed $100 to the American Missionary Association "to be appropriated for the education of the freedmen and their women and children." His antislavery views were not shared by many in eastern Maine; abolitionists were limited mainly to fervent Christians such as Holyoke, who was the first president of the Brewer First Congregational Church.

Fannie Pearson Hardy was born in Brewer on June 18, 1865, the daughter of Manly and Emeline Wheeler Hardy. She graduated from Smith College and served as superintendent of the Brewer school system from 1889 to 1891. After marrying Rev. Jacob Eckstorm in 1893, she wrote numerous books on Penobscot Indian lore under the name Fannie Hardy Eckstorm. James B. Vickery of the renowned perfectionist wrote, "She was a lady of firm convictions but whose accuracy in historical matters is dependable."

Ornithology, the study of birds, was only one of the topics that intrigued Manly Hardy, whose daughter Fannie was the best known of his five children. Through his trading with Native Americans, he learned their language and garnered their trust. The gifted woodsman, trapper, and canoeist was well acquainted with the North Maine Woods. Fannie once lamented, "By the greater part of his information and almost all of his rich experience in the woods never were committed to paper."

Young Fannie Hardy often accompanied her father on woods excursions, visiting lumber camps where she held her own with the roughest of characters, all the while absorbing their habits and manner of speech for such classic books as *Penobscot Man,* published in 1904. This portrait from the Maine Folklife Center pictures her displaying what might have been that evening's dinner meal and maybe a specimen for study. She shared her father's love of wild birds, writing *The Bird Book,* a text for children, and *The Woodpeckers.* She died in 1945.

Sculptor Charles Eugene Tefft, born in Brewer in 1874, poses with a bust of Julius Caesar that he created as a teenager. His brother, Nathan A. Tefft, wrote that Charles copied the bust from one loaned to him by the Bangor Historical Society. "As he rode through the streets in the back of a rickety express cart, holding and hugging Julius tightly in his arms," wrote Nathan, "he was the curiosity, if not the envy, of a small army of boys who followed him." When one boy said that Caesar was dead, Charles shot back, "I'll make him live again."

The Tefft family home at 235 Center Street is now the headquarters of the Veterans of Foreign Wars Post No. 4917. Charles Tefft's grandfather was Rev. Benjamin E. Tefft. His father was Henry Tefft and his mother was Eliza Parsons. The mansion was built in 1837 by Dr. Horatio N. Page. It was purchased by the Teffts c. 1865.

This later photograph shows Charles E. Tefft (left) and an assistant sculpting a statue of Hannibal Hamlin in 1927. The statue stands in the Kenduskeag Mall in downtown Bangor, the home town of Hamlin, who served as Abraham Lincoln's first vice president from 1861 to 1865. Tefft also sculpted the River Drivers memorial, the bronze Victory statue, the Florence Bragg Bird Foundation, all located in Bangor, in addition to a memorial fountain in the Bronx and a war memorial on Staten Island. Of his brother's lesser known penchant for the great outdoors, brother Nathan Tefft wrote, "If one is fortunate enough to be along with him, whether it be fishing from a boat on Sebec Lake, or frying venison and onions in the wilds of Old Katahdin, he will find it, as it has been to me, a pleasure and an inspiration."

Clara E. Farrington helped spread her pioneering family name outside of New England. Following the Civil War, she taught at an institution for freed slaves called a freedman school, located in South Carolina. The patriarch of the family was John Farrington, who immigrated to the District of Maine in 1786, clearing land in the Wrentham Settlement of Holden. He often spoke of the joys and sorrows of pioneer living.

Another member of the Farrington family took her knowledge and education even farther than Clara. Sarah Farrington taught at Robert College in Turkey, truly a remarkable achievement for a woman in the 19th century. She was married to William A. Perkins. In the 20th century, her relative, Albert Farrington, operated a photographic studio in the Burr Block at 3 State Street, near the Bangor-Brewer Bridge. The name Farrington was spread around eastern Maine as much by his portrait work as any other means.

Six

HOUSES OF WORSHIP

Parishioners have long been inspired by this beautiful stained-glass window located in the front of the First United Methodist Church of Brewer. Named "Christ, the Shepherd," the window was designed by Spence, Bell & Company of Boston in memory of members Joseph Shackley, Frank Collins, and James Mayo. The company also created other windows for the building's dedication on January 15, 1905.

Joshua Lawrence Chamberlain was only one of the people in attendance at the dedication of this preeminent Brewer landmark, the First Congregational church, on March 28, 1890. There is still a "Chamberlain family pew" inside the hillside edifice where one can sit and absorb a bit of history. After parishioners voted in 1889 to build a larger church, the former church located on the same site was cut in two, hauled to the lower end of Church Street, and set up as two apartment houses.

Missionaries were the backbone of church outreach programs. The First Congregational Church sponsored Rev. and Mrs. Pease, who followed Rev. Benjamin Snow as missionaries to Micronesia. These people were truly pioneers, going into the wilderness with only their faith, their Bibles, and the good wishes of parishioners back home.

The Second Congregational Church in South Brewer, not far from the Orrington town line, came about after the First Congregational Church in town became overcrowded. The church has stood in its present location since late 1846. It was rededicated on January 7, 1906, around the time the photograph for this postcard was taken, after the chapel at the right was attached to the main building.

The predecessor to the present First Congregational church was this building, which faced down the river beside the town hall, built on an adjoining lot. People far down the Penobscot River could see the two buildings standing on what was known as Meeting House Hill. This structure was built in 1828, dedicated in 1829, remodeled in 1835, enlarged in 1878, and removed in 1889.

The stone walls of the 1905 First Methodist church stood in stark contrast to traditional church construction in eastern Maine. Some felt the building was more medieval in appearance than other buildings, the church having a tower on its northeast corner and a large window arch facing South Main Street. On January 15, 1955, marking the golden anniversary of the building's dedication, parishioners burned the mortgage on the loan needed to repair the tower.

The original Methodist church, located on the same lot as the later building, was erected in 1853 at a cost of $3,000. The pulpit was at the rear of the church, while the organ and choir were at the opposite end toward Main Street. Pews were rented for $5 to $15 per year, according to their location. The vestry at right was completed in 1887. The final service inside the old church, which was due for demolition after being condemned, was on April 2, 1903.

New Baptist Church Brewer dedication 1909

The members of Brewer's First Baptist congregation pose for the dedication of their new building on October 3, 1909. The church was founded on October 22, 1885, by 26 members of the Columbia Street Baptist Church in Bangor who were dismissed so they could worship across the river. The congregation grew during the years that services were held in a public hall. Membership had risen to 121 members when this photograph was taken. The First Baptist church, renamed Calvary Baptist in 1933, remained the city's only Baptist edifice until 1987, when the Twin City Baptist Church was built in North Brewer.

Calvary Baptist's large pipe organ has long filled the sanctuary with sacred music, most notably during Christmas and Easter services, normally days of peak attendance. Since its construction, the church has been enlarged and modernized several times. Most notable was the addition of classroom space on the Jordan Street side. The congregation's first minister was Rev. W.E. Lombard, who began preaching in July 1896 and stayed two years.

The dedication of the new St. Teresa's Catholic church in August 1948 was a joyous occasion for all the parishioners, who were still saddened by the destruction by fire of the wooden church across the street. A driving force behind the construction of the new sandstone-colored church was Rev. Morris Carroll, who was the pastor at the time of the fire. Pictured is the laying of the cornerstone, which was blessed by the Most Reverend Daniel J. Feeney of Portland.

The old St. Teresa's church in South Brewer was destroyed on November 6, 1945. Construction of the wooden building began in 1894 to serve the town's growing Catholic population. In 1896, the parish was born, growing rapidly into the next century.

Religious matters rarely make the front pages of daily newspapers. However, this 1948 view of the Most Reverend Feeney (center) walking with Rev. Francis LeTourneau of Orono and Rev. H. Francis Cox of St. Mary's Church in Bangor, was deemed too important by *Bangor Daily News* editors to run it anywhere else. The only element lacking was color to highlight the colorful robes worn by the participants.

Confirmation Day in May 1959 at St. Teresa's church was an occasion of great ceremony and solemnity. The altar boys had learned their lessons well, both in the church and at the St. Teresa's School down the street. Identified in the rear are Father Houlihan in the high black hat, and Monsignor Hogan behind, facing to the left.

In 1981, a bronze bell believed to be more than a century old was hoisted into place at the new St. Joseph's Catholic church on North Main Street. The Reverend Richard E. Harvey purchased the bell from the Archdiocese of New York and had it installed on four laminated wooden beams. A plaque mentions the generosity of church member Michael Eremita in installing the bell.

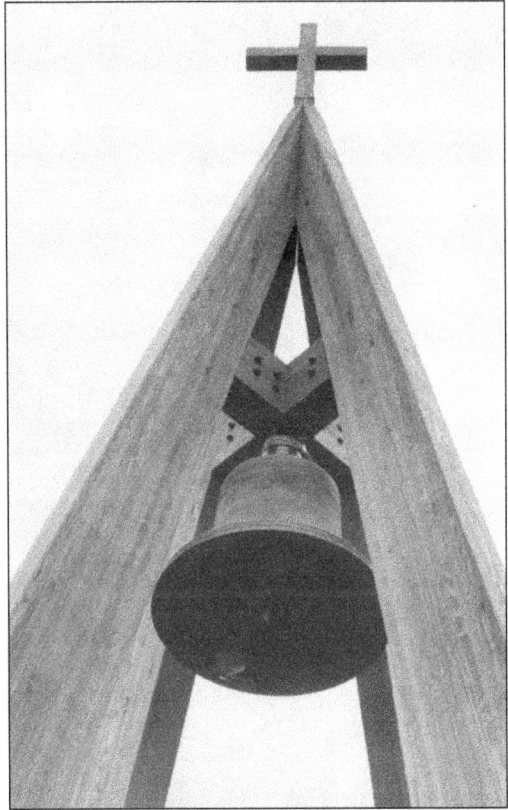

St. Joseph's Catholic church was completed in October 1926 to serve worshippers who had tired of traveling to South Brewer and to Bangor for services. The Reverend Thomas Moriarity was long associated with St. Joseph's, a wooden edifice located at North Main and Holyoke Streets. Members of St. Patrick's Episcopal Church celebrated their first Eucharist here on September 14, 1975, after St. Joseph's vacated the property and built a new church farther out North Main Street.

The hearty smile and generous spirit of Rev. E. Charles Dartnell, pastor of the First United Methodist of Brewer from 1946 to 1962, were remembered long after his death in 1981. The dynamic British-born pastor was in constant demand for graduation and baccalaureate addresses. A Brewer apartment complex was named in his memory.

A winter view of the First Methodist church shows its graceful but sturdy design. Its cornerstone was laid on July 17, 1903. Construction costs totaled about $16,000, more than five times that of the former church that it replaced. The building and its grounds have retained their beauty despite advancing age and the encroachment of commercial development on all sides.

Seven

LEISURE-TIME ACTIVITIES

The white houses, the crowds leaning over the wooden fence, and the whir of the rubber-lined wheels on the pavement were all so familiar to anyone who ever attended a soapbox derby race. That stretch of State Street is also well paved as the summertime event approaches. It has been long sponsored by the *Bangor Daily News*, which published action photographs such as this one in its Monday editions.

The key to the success of the soapbox derby races was having Maine businesses sponsor the boys' racing vehicles. The businessman on the right is from Caribou, Maine, in Aroostook County. Many racers from "the County" and their families made the trek to Brewer every year to root for their sons, grandsons, or maybe the kid next-door.

The Bacon and Robinson fuel company sponsored this young racer, c. 1948. He seems to be getting plenty of advice from a pipe-smoking businessman and members of his family—and in the hallway of his home, no less. In 1955 and 1956, two brothers were back-to-back winners. They were LeRoy and Dick Crawford of Holden, Maine.

82

This dramatic photograph shows the starting ramp during the final heat of the 1949 *Bangor Daily News*–Chevrolet Soap Box Derby. Racing down State Street, with the Brewer Auditorium in the distance on the left, are Sonny Averill of Prentiss, Maine, (left) and Bill Houghton. Houghton, whose race car was sponsored by Houghton Cedar Products Company of Lee, won the grand championship.

John Bouchard of Millinocket, winner of the 1962 soapbox derby, is congratulated by his mother, Rose Murphy Bouchard, and his father, Ernest Bouchard, who sponsored his son in the event. At the national soapbox derby championship in Akron, Ohio, John won the first heat before losing in the second round. He went to become a successful accountant, typifying the productive lives many derby winners led as adults.

The names Kiah, Baker, Hackett, Lebrun, and Pendleton came to be familiar to spectators at Eastern Park on South Main Street, where the Eastern AA Baseball teams played many a summer night. In 1919, the club won 11 out of 19 starts and lost 7, and one game was in the ninth inning when the Newport manager refused to abide by the umpire's decision when the score stood at 4–4.

Sponsored by the Eastern Fine Paper company, the Eastern baseball team knew how to warm up a crowd in the days before television and visits to Fenway Park brought professional baseball up close and personal. Somewhere in this group is baseball star Billy Kiah, about whom historian Howard Kenney wrote in 1989, "Billy knew the game as good as anyone, and he played in the same fashion. [He was] Eastern all the way."

Brewer High School's baseball club, *c.* 1925, also entertained crowds. Note the letter *B* on the white uniforms, as well as the white caps, and the long canvas bat bag in front with the team's name stamped onto it. Also, the two men standing, probably high school teachers doubling as team managers, are wearing straw hats known as boaters, popular during the 1920s.

Another group portrait of the same vintage shows a larger team posing indoors, but with a similarly serious "let's go out and get 'em" expression. The uniforms and gloves probably wouldn't pass muster with the school's well-equipped team of today.

This action photograph from the October 28–29, 1944 edition of the *Bangor Daily News* was published in anticipation of a contest at 2 p.m. Saturday with Bangor's John Bapst High School team. The newspaper reported, "The game, which on paper shapes up as a bitterly contested affair all the way, will mark the resumption of athletic relations between the schools after a break that lasted 10 years."

This joyous occasion, in February 1960, happened at the Bangor Auditorium after the Brewer Witches beat the Presque Isle Wildcats for the Eastern L basketball title. The score was 85–59. Star player Danny Coombs scored 39 points that evening. Pictured are band members and other students following the victory.

Another view following the 1960 victory tells it all. The team members undoubtedly are chanting, "We're No. 1, we're No. 1!" along with a packed Bangor Auditorium house. The player at the left, holding the treasured plaque, is wearing the traditional basket string that he and his teammates have just pulled down. Sports columnist Bud Leavitt wrote, "A combination of Coombs, Dennis (The Menace) Vanidestine, Alan Leathers, Dave Farley and Palmer Little blended beautifully to provide Brewer with a dynamic attack and rock-ribbed defense."

An undated photograph from the archive of the Brewer Public Library, probably from the 1930s, shows the girls' high school basketball team. Note the serious facial expressions. Little could they have imagined the popularity girls' basketball has gained at Brewer and other schools in recent years.

Fourth of July parades were eagerly anticipated each year. This procession on North Main Street, heading toward the Wilson Street intersection, shows two pumper trucks from the fire department, and the tail end of a horse-drawn ladder truck at the left. Historian Howard Kenney recalls the abundance of firecrackers and torpedoes, many of which were manufactured at the torpedo factory located in North Brewer.

A summertime view shows a trio of boys eyeing an ice cream vendor. Around 1910, lower Wilson Street, between Main Street and the Penobscot River, was lined with wooden buildings that were razed half a century later, when the street was widened during the construction of the Joshua Chamberlain toll bridge. Thompson Print shop was housed in the dark building on the left. Across the dirt street, a store sold ice cream soda and cigars.

This Fourth of July parade picture shows children and adults on North Street and a straight-shouldered firefighter driving a fire pumper, drawn by two white horses. Historian Howard Kenney recalls, "On State Street, from the bridge, to the junction of State and Wilson Streets, there was a flag flying at every house." That cannot be said of today's holiday celebrations.

The Hose No. 5 team from South Brewer poses on July 4, 1909. A man dressed as Uncle Sam, and another as a clown add levity to the festivities. The round vehicle behind the team is one of the hose carts used in the heated competition with other teams from throughout Maine.

This photograph shows a Boy Scout troop on May 20, 1921. Troop No. 1 was formed at the First Congregational church in 1909, predating by a year the official chartering of the national Boy Scouts. In 1920, the Bangor-Brewer local Boy Scout Council was chartered and the Brewer Congregational Troop was formed.

George Hayes, a patriotic member of Troop No. 1 Boy Scouts, salutes Lt. Burton Weil of Drexel Hill, Pennsylvania, a World War II-era pilot stationed at Dow Field in Bangor. The 11-year-old scout, who participated in metal scrap drives and other civilian defense programs, was visiting the air base when a newspaper photographer took his picture, published July 7, 1942. A former scout, Weil remembered earnestly taking the Boy Scout oath.

The Brewer Boy Scouts was still a young organization when the members posed for this portrait on Memorial Day 1911. A month earlier, while the Great Fire was raging in Bangor, Troop No. 1 joined the National Guard and University of Maine ROTC cadets in patrolling the city streets. Under strict orders not to let anyone into the burning city, the scouts barred all people lacking special police permits, including Gov. Frederick S. Plaisted. The governor nonetheless recognized them with a citation for community service.

Life was not always serious for the Brewer scouts. On a summer day in the 1920s, a group poses while on a camping trip in an open automobile. For comic relief, one of the older boys holds up a frying pan. The Reverend Basil Gleason and Merrill Dooey are standing on the left.

Photo by Dan Maher

Heavyweight boxing champion Jack Dempsey poses with an unidentified angler at North Brewer, where he was hosted in 1933 by members of the Penobscot Salmon Club. Older men present were reminded of the young fighter's boxing match at Eastern Park in South Brewer on the night of July 28, 1922. Needless to say, he won the contest.

Beginning in 1912, a rite of spring was to catch the first fresh-run salmon of the year at the Bangor Salmon Pool (actually approached from North Brewer), and have it shipped to the White House. In 1943, the lucky angler was Adolf Fischer of Brewer (left), who landed a "20-pounder." Pictured with Fischer is fellow fisherman Harold Hatch. U.S. marshal John G. Utterback purchased the fish for $3 a pound and had it shipped to President Franklin D. Roosevelt.

Eight

PAPER, LUMBER, BRICKS, AND ICE

For more than a century, the plume of smoke from Eastern Fine Paper in South Brewer has meant stability and prosperity for untold families, and for the city in general. Fred Ayer bought the Palmer and Johnson pulp mill in the 1880s, expanding the mill's capacity and adding three more band saws. He later converted a part of the lumber mill into a producer of manila and wrapping paper. Today it is known for its fine business papers.

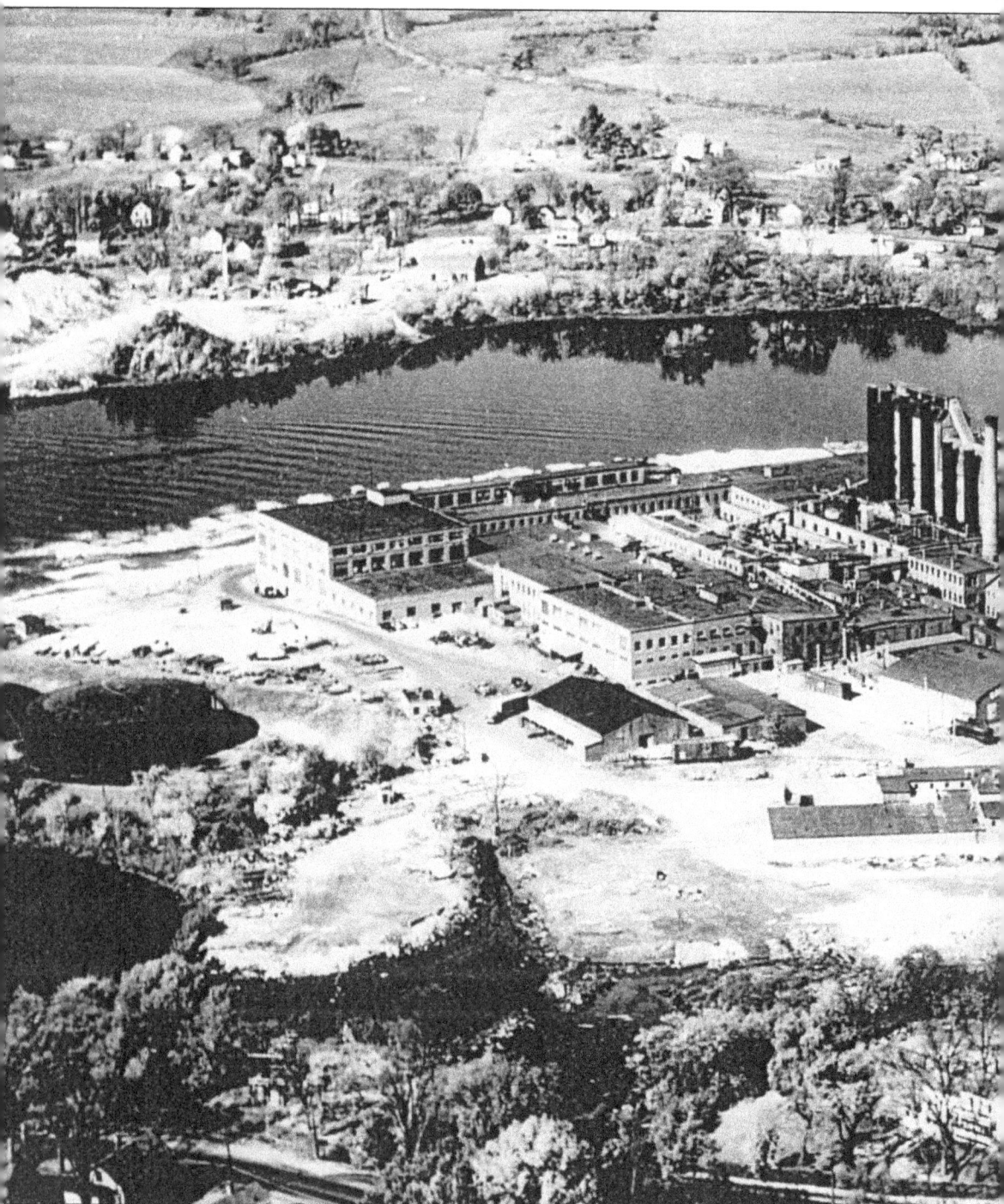

This 1952 aerial view shows the mill property that has dominated the lower Penobscot River and South Brewer for generations. Both rag-content and chemical wood fiber papers were first manufactured here, especially after Fred Ayer shut down the sawmill part of the operation in 1916 and concentrated solely on the paper manufacturing. Fortunately, Ayer stayed abreast of

new paper-making techniques. Of great importance was a new method of producing pulp from hardwood. Another factor was the available millions of water each day from Brewer Lake. It was needed for use in clean, white paper production. Much has changed on the river and beyond, but the mill continues its reputation for fine paper products.

Today, the Occupational Safety and Health Administration (OSHA) would take a dim view of these working conditions. Women are sorting rags while inhaling chemical fumes from open barrels at the Eastern mill. This rarely seen photograph (and the three following pictures) were selected from a *c.* 1921 photograph album that was given to the city clerk's office by Arthur Tilley, long associated with the Eastern mill.

This view shows hazardous working conditions that probably raised few concerns in the 1920s. The Eastern Electro-Chemical Company was organized in 1916 to manufacture bleach liquor for the mill. It was absorbed in the Eastern Manufacturing Company in 1920. That same year, Stuart W. Webb assumed direction of the company and its subsidiaries, which included the Lincoln Pulpwood Company in Lincoln, Maine.

One can only guess as to the circumstances in this photograph, labeled simply "cutting up rags." The male worker carries a pile of cloth in his left hand, having lost his right arm. In the background two women work at a large paper machine. A landmark year at the mill was 1940, when the Kanyr Bleaching system was introduced, providing an improved quality of rayon in paper pulp.

"Putting pulpwood into pond" is the title of this dramatic photograph taken c. 1921. The pond, as these workers knew it, no longer exists. In 1950, Eastern produced an astonishing 72,223 tons of pulp, of which 47,163 tons were converted into paper. The mill was operating on a full six-day production schedule throughout the year—quite a change from the early days of Joab Palmer and Benjamin Johnson.

The Sargent Lumber Company was the town's oldest lumber manufacturing plant, being an outgrowth of a gristmill and sawmill built by Col. John Brewer in 1784. Workers are pictured in South Brewer amidst rafts and lumber piles along the riverbank. At one time, Sargent interests contributed much of the business and industrial activities in that part of Brewer.

This World War II-era landing barge—dubbed the LCVP by soldiers who invaded the beaches of Normandy and other ports more than half a century ago—unloads pulpwood for use at the Eastern Fine Paper mill, probably in the late 1940s. Note the wooden booms to the port and starboard side of the ship, used in early lumbering days to tie up rafts of logs. Much pulp is still resting at the bottom of the Penobscot.

Laborers at the D. Sargent's Sons lumber mill hold the tools of their trade for a portrait from the late 1800s. A worker holds an ax handle, and behind him another man holds a peavey, invented by Joe Peavey, a local man. The name of the mill was changed to the Sargent Lumber Company in 1902 with Daniel A. Sergeant, the son of the late founder, named vice president and general manager.

An expansive view of the company from the same era shows the rambling buildings and wooden wagons used to transport lumber overland. Also, railroad tracks facilitate transportation of another variety. The Sargent family helped build Brewer into a strong community. Daniel Sargent came to the area from Massachusetts. Later, they were early investors in the Eastern corporation.

It was often said that Bangor lumber and Brewer brick built the large cities in the years of urban growth in the mid-to-late 19th century. Pictured in August 1939 are the crew of the Brooks Brick Company, one of several brickyards that put Brewer on the map. They are celebrating the manufacture of 55,000 bricks in 8.5 hours, a record production.

Brewer bricks were on great demand in cities such as Boston, which had suffered from the great fire of 1872, and others along the eastern seaboard. Much of the Beacon Hill district is said to have been constructed of these bricks. An 1857 newspaper article noted the decline of Bangor's brick-making operations and the rise of Brewer's. Apparently the clay was of higher quality on that side of the river.

In 1906, Dr. George Tibbetts, John Elmer Littlefield, and Harrison N. Brooks bought the Hugh O'Brien yard and incorporated it as the Brooks Brick Company. Located at the end of Maple Street, the yard consisted of 35 acres. This picture shows the Brewer Brick Cart on the far left, a conveyance constructed with two wheels to facilitate the easy sliding of the bricks.

Another view of the Brooks yard shows the large shed under construction. The business is still located in Brewer, but no longer manufactures the bricks that it wholesales. Three brickyards were located in town before 1850. The one operated by Elbridge Harlow turned out 600,000 bricks in one year. Brooks' kiln shed had a holding capacity of 2 million bricks.

The planing mill operated by James H. Smith comprised several acres on the highlands bordering the Penobscot River. Smith rebuilt the prosperous business after an 1882 fire destroyed the buildings. Some 20 years later, however, it burned again. An 1893 advertisement described the business as dealers in long and short lumber, a variety of planing "done in the best manner and at shortest notice."

Smith Planing Mill workers, accompanied by a couple of children, take a break from sawing and planing to pose for a group portrait. The mill was incorporated in 1882, the year of the first fire. During a portion of the season, the company manufactured box boards for use in the construction of shipping cases for various manufacturing firms. Shingles, clapboards, and laths also were made there.

Workers are shown cutting the ice near the Rollins icehouse at the end of Wilson Street. On the first freezing of the river the owners of the various ice plants staked out their space. Normally cutting began by the first of January, lasting a month to six weeks. One year, nature did not cooperate, and cutting was delayed until February 15, diminishing the profit made by the different companies.

The Getchell Brothers ice company was strictly a horse-and-wagon operation in its early years, unlike the modern business, aided by electric refrigeration, operated today by the Farnham family. Getchell cut much of its ice on the Kendusekag Stream in Bangor, even opening an office near the business district. Mildred Thayer, like children everywhere, used to follow the wagon, snatch up the pieces of ice, and eat them.

The crew working the west end paper machine at the Eastern Fine Paper mill in South Brewer poses in this c. 1935 photograph. From left to right are Dan Tardiff, Lew Dupray, Lee Debeck, and Bert Buck. Wide shoulders, strong backs, and nerves of steel were required to work the big machines. The hours were long, but the work was steady and the pay reasonable for the Depression years. It seems everyone in Brewer is related to, or knows someone, who worked in the mill in its more than 100 years of operation.

This state-of-the-art icehouse and elevator was located on South Main Street. Cutting, storing, and transporting ice was a dangerous, tricky business. The job was dirty and cold, and workers had to have their wits about them to avoid serious injury. As each ice cake entered the elevator it passed under a knife that removed the "snow ice" and cut the cake to a uniform depth of 12 inches.

Nine

ACTS OF GOD

A massive wall of ice in the March flood of 1902 tore out the middle span of the old covered bridge. Not since the spring flood of 1846, when the first covered bridge across the Penobscot River was destroyed, had residents been so terrified by nature's fury. One newspaper reported, "It was an astonishing and unforgettable sight to see the wreckage moving down on the river amid the ice."

This odd sight greeted travelers passing between Bangor and Brewer in the months following the spring flood of 1902. Since the bridge was the only way for teams of horses and other vehicles to pass between the twin cities, this makeshift span was crucial to maintain day-to-day activities.

Historian Edward Foley recounted the 1902 disaster in an essay written for a 1989 history of Brewer. "Irresistible as it come down [the river], a mountain of ice hit, first the railroad bridge and a moment later, the Bangor-Brewer Bridge," he wrote. "Both center sections were taken out as the ice-mass swept by."

The Bangor Bridge Company was formed to repair the gaping hole in the bridge's center section. Perhaps these well-dressed men are representatives of the company, planning the steel span which eventually replaced this temporary section. The strange-looking steel and wood hybrid stood until 1912, when the all-steel bridge familiar to modern-day motorists today was finally built.

The old wooden truss of the damaged bridge is very evident in this unusual photograph, looking toward the Brewer shore. The toll was finally removed from the bridge when its center span was replaced by steel. Work on the all-steel bridge was started on October 28, 1911. It measured 658 feet long and seemed modern compared to the old wooden structure that had stood longer than anyone could remember.

Flotsam and jetsam from a spring flood, probably in 1923, is strewn across the Brewer waterfront near the old iron bridge. Part of a boat lies abandoned in the river, along with lumber no doubt deposited on the shore from one of the many riverfront mills. Railroad cars sit idle on the Bangor shore in the distance, at far left. That city sustained substantial property damage, owing to flooding of the Kenduskeag Stream that bisects the business district.

On several occasions during the 20th century, surging river water hurled mammoth ice cakes onto Route 9, which has been nicknamed the Airline Road since stagecoach days owing to its comparatively direct route to Calais, Maine, 90 miles to the east. An armed guard stands watch in this photograph, most likely taken during the March 1936 spring freshet. A man on the extreme right, perhaps a nearby resident, surveys the devastation.

108

Veteran grocer Daniel Rooney stands just above the waterline in this undated photograph, perhaps taken during the 1936 flooding. Rooney operated the shop at North Main and Burr Streets from 1897 until his retirement in 1947, when his son, James, took over the business. The elder Rooney was no stranger to cresting tides. After the middle section of the Bangor-Brewer Bridge was swept away in the 1902 flood, he drove a horse with a load of groceries over the temporary span.

A newspaper photographer captured this hapless man struggling along Route 9, then called the Eddington Road. This picture was published on March 28, 1936. Residents living near the racing river moved whatever belongings they could carry to higher ground. Spectators watched anxiously as ice cakes crashed against each other with such force that destruction of a tiny white house seemed inevitable. The structure escaped destruction.

This fire at the Studebaker Service Station on South Main Street drew throngs of bystanders expecting to witness the barnlike structure's roof collapsing. It did not collapse, but there was still plenty of excitement as firefighters laid down hoses along the dirt road leading to the riverfront building. Dated sometime in the early 1920s, the picture shows early automobiles parked beside horse-drawn fire apparatus.

The burning of the Rollins icehouses on July 27, 1906, was immortalized in hand-colored penny postcards that today are snatched up by antique collectors fascinated by the high drama that they depict. A lighted cigar stub or cigarette discarded in dry grass near the Hathorn Manufacturing Company ignited the inferno, which claimed $70,000 worth of property. Also charred were a Wilson Street dwelling and lumber supplies.

Eleven families, including 30 children, fled to safety on July 18, 1960, as flames damaged this apartment block on Fling Street. The near tragedy included a 10-month-old girl who was snatched from her crib seconds before flames burst through the ceiling. The 12 members of the Linwood Wickett family lost most of their possessions. Photographer Spike Webb took this photograph and another one showing off-duty Bangor fireman Frank Harding, a store clerk, fighting the blaze in a white shirt and bow tie.

Members of Brewer's all-volunteer fire department toiled long hours battling this stubborn blaze at the Connor Coal & Wood Company on South Main Street, opposite Spring Street. The small office building at the center was burned, behind which was a curious overhead trolley used for delivery onto ships in the river just out of view in the distance.

The only two victims of the Great Bangor Fire of April 30, 1911, were Brewer residents John N. Scribner, age 70, and George Abbott, 41. Scribner, a shoemaker, walked across the bridge to survey the devastation when he was trapped under a collapsing office building, visible at the center of this photograph. Volunteer firefighter Abbott perished while battling a house fire on Penobscot Street.

Brewer fire historian Paul E. Tower has identified this classic old photograph showing Hose No. 2 firehouse on Parker Street, near the site of the present-day water district. Taken sometime between 1910 and 1915, it shows the shiny steamer that was a favorite with children at Fourth of July parades. The building was also called Central Fire Station. Unlike today's fire department—which supplements volunteer firefighters with a full-time, salaried staff—the old force was largely volunteer. Even the little white mascot worked for free.

The upper echelon of the Brewer Fire Department in bygone days was a serious-looking group, ready to tackle any blaze, and there were many to tackle in the years before smoke alarms and fire codes. The man on the far right of the first row was Lt. Frank Moore, the uncle of historian Mildred N. Thayer. She writes that the large bell in the belfry of the city hall alerted residents and firefighters of disaster. The bell was inaudible in some parts of town; in 1901, a whistle-type electric telegraph system was installed with a total of 10 boxes.

A carelessly tossed firecracker reportedly started an Independence Day fire near the waterfront in 1924. Brewer's new American LaFrance fire pumper was pressed into service, under the supervision of fire chief Irving "Dickie" Doyle, shown standing on the left (Doyle is also pictured on page 122). Navy men from the two ships anchored in Bangor were ferried over to fight blazes at the Smart and Bartlett Livery Stable, Lane's Blacksmith Shop and Johnston's Bakery.

Photographer John C. Thayer savored the opportunity to capture a drama on film. This undated, unidentified photograph from the Mildred N. Thayer collection shows fire apparatus near Thayer's studio at 21 North Main Street. Fire historian Paul E. Tower has pointed out the contrast between the horse-drawn apparatus on the right and the motorized fire truck on the left, possibly dating the photograph to the 1920s.

Spectators sprinted to the riverfront on September 1, 1906, to watch the burning of the *Annie L. Henderson*, the sails and rigging of which caught fire while it was tied up at a Bangor wharf. A nearby coal fire ignited the vessel, which was swept across to the Brewer shore by a stiff wind. The schooner was then towed to the middle of the river, where it smoldered throughout the day and night.

Ten

POSTCARDS AND
SNAPSHOTS

An electric streetcar rumbles through the intersection of South Main and Wilson Streets in this *c.* 1930 postcard view while Hazen Danforth Sr. pumps water from a much used public well. The Good Gulf gasoline pumps in front of the Danforth Hardware Store also saw lots of activity. None of the buildings pictured stands today; a Brooks Pharmacy now occupies the site of the large wooden block at left.

Holyoke Square at North Main and Center Streets was not even paved when this photograph was taken. A few old automobiles pass by local businesses. The Patten Black at the right was an early location of the Brewer Savings Bank. Also in the neighborhood were William Seeley's print shop and Norman Hall's grocery. The smokestack may have belonged to the Smith Planing Mill on the river.

Center Street is still a busy thoroughfare, a popular route from Brewer across the new Penobscot Bridge to Bangor. Around 1915, it was a tidy row of businesses, including Victor Hinkley's drugstore on the corner, with Adolphus Beaupre's bicycle shop doing a brisk business at 99 Center Street. Today, these places exist only in our memories, as does the large elm in the background.

116

Sam Wyman, the tuba-playing South Brewer native, used to show postcards like this one to skeptics who argued the city never had a bandstand. It was located on the lawn beside the First Congregational church. The present city hall stands near the site of the old hall on Church Street. Their symmetrical proportions made the two landmarks a popular subject for photographers.

Countless memories went up in flames the day the old city hall was destroyed in March 1937. The building had housed early high school classes. The building, writes historian Howard F. Kenney, even had jail cells in addition to the city clerk's office and city council meeting rooms. A stage was much used across the south end of a meeting room on the top floor. The rafters also resonated with the sounds of the fireman's ball, church fairs, and boxing matches.

St. Teresa's Catholic church forms a picturesque backdrop in this fine old postcard, postmarked September 27, 1909. Close inspection will find a well-dressed couple sitting in the buggy, heading out of South Brewer toward Orrington. Might it be their wedding day? The wooden church burned on November 6, 1945.

Before the luxury of paved streets, sprinkling carts were pressed into surface in dry weather to "lay down" the dust. This photograph shows George Hinman and his two gray horses on North Main Street. The Carter Block, home of the Brewer Savings Bank for many years, is in the background. In extremely hot, dry weather, the South Brewer truck driver probably refilled the large barrel many times before completing his task.

This old postcard bears the title "A So. Brewer Jitney," which would suggest this mule-drawn carriage was for hire and was apparently hired by the elderly woman seated behind the driver. The slope of the hill suggests the picture was taken on upper Brewer Street. The term *jitney* may be derived from the French *jeton*, meaning *token*.

Winter scenes from the early 20th century are uncommon because of the time and trouble required to set up photographic equipment. But J. Craig Thayer, whose studio was located just out of the right range of this photograph, was never one to let weather stand in the way of a good picture. Winter road care was first mentioned in 1836, when the town voted that highway surveyors should keep the roads broken out during the winter. This view shows horse-drawn wagons and a streetcar on North Main Street near Wilson Street.

J. Craig Thayer, who took this and many other street scenes in this book, had a photographic studio visible near the right side of this picture. The winter day he took this photograph, a snowplow had already broken a path up the middle of North Main Street. Thayer's daughter, Mildred N. Thayer, writes that in the 19th century, men who worked on clearing the roads were to receive $1 a day for their services. This was to come out of the next year's taxes. The surveyors were directed to purchase a machine to break out the roads.

BRIMMER SQ. BREWER.

This old postcard, courtesy of collector and antique dealer John LaFountain, bears this pencil-written note, written with more than a trace of sarcasm: "Brewer on a busy day." Brimmer Square at Wilson and Main Streets was normally quite busy, with traffic coming from all directions. Street paving in the city began in 1908–1909 with 375 feet of macadamized road, beginning at Center Street. The pavement was later continued 1,310 feet to Brimmer Street, making dusty scenes like this a thing of the past.

Wood & Huggard Undertakers, located on the hill at 255 North Main Street, advertised "the most complete line of goods east of Boston," as well as a "chapel for funerals free of charge." From left to right are Harvard H. Clark standing by the ambulance, Frederick K. Huggard by the Model T Ford, and hearse driver Joseph E. Huggard.

A panoramic view of Brewer, c. 1885, shows a city of tidy white, wooden homes stretching as far as the eye can see. Perhaps photographer J.G. Jackman lugged his equipment to the top of the First Congregational church to capture his town in all its glory. At the center, to the left of the flagpole, is the old church vestry. After the third church was built in 1890, the building was used as a post office until it burned.

Built at a cost of $64,996.14 and completed on November 8, 1939, the Brewer Auditorium continues to serve the city as its foremost municipal meeting place. Nicknamed "the house that FDR built" because its construction was funded with Depression-era government relief money, the brick structure has hosted basketball tournaments, the Daniel E. Geagan American Legion Post No. 98, and dances featuring rock and roll musicians Bill Haley and His Comets.

The Irving T. Doyle athletic field beside the auditorium was dedicated with a flurry of speeches and fireworks on July 4, 1948. Named in memory of former fire chief, businessman, and sports enthusiast "Dickie" Doyle, who had died eight months previously, the field has been the scene of many heated football rivalries.

Work on the new armory on Elm Street in South Brewer was started on April 28, 1941, and was completed on February 28, 1942. It replaced the wooden structure on South Main Street, which was formerly a fire station, and was converted to an armory when all fire apparatus was moved to the central station with the modernization of that department. New construction was rare during the resource-scarce war years, but armories were deemed essential to the war effort and sprouted throughout the country.

Dedication ceremonies of the new Brewer Public Library were held on September 27, 1966. Former librarian Constance Holling has traced the institution's history back to 1907, when 30 people met in the old city hall to discuss the feasibility of establishing a library. On October 14, 1907, the Brewer Free Public Library Association was born. Today's paid staff was preceded by volunteer aides under the supervision of Fannie Hardy Eckstorm, followed by several others, including Frances Constantine, the first full-time librarian, in 1946.

The Dirigo Running Team was photographed in front of their new Hose No. 3 firehouse near South Main and Burr Streets in 1898. Team members formed a little band, marching on holidays, but they were best known for Fourth of July and Labor Day competitions with other firefighting teams in the Penobscot River Valley. Running out the hose was serious business, requiring synchronization and lots of practice. On one occasion in its earliest years, Fourth of July refreshments included half a barrel of beer, 50 cigars, and a quart of whiskey.

Members of a brass band carry their instruments back into town after performing at Oak Hill Cemetery on South Main Street. The date is c. 1920. The occasion is probably a ceremony honoring Decoration Day, later renamed Memorial Day. Bands traditionally assembled at ceremonies honoring the dead in the old burial ground, the final resting place of Col. John Brewer and the Holyoke and Chamberlain families.

In 1924, a far different kind of parade was staged. Dozens of members of the Ku Klux Klan marched down South Main Street garbed in their traditional white hoods and flowing robes. An estimated 150,000 Maine residents belonged to the KKK in the mid-1920s, rivaling any southern state. Because of a scarcity of African Americans in Maine, the KKK was largely anti-Catholic and anti-Jewish, a sobering fact for the ethnic populations in South Brewer and in Bangor, where the KKK owned a "klavern," or meeting hall.

The "klansmen" paraded with a wooden cross, an American flag, and other insignia while pedestrians on Main Street looked on. During the KKK's first daylight march in the nation in 1923, bystanders in Milo, Maine, identified marchers from the color of their shoes. One little girl spotted her father's footwear and ran alongside him, much to his chagrin. Some 20,000 KKK robes were sold in Maine at this time. The group eventually fell apart due to its own excesses and power struggles.

Actress Joan Crawford, fourth from left, attends the 1959 opening of the Rudman Beverage Company plant on Wilson Street, accompanied by Herbert L. Barnet, far left, president of Pepsi-Cola. Crawford's late husband, Al Steele, had been Pepsi's chairman of the board and she was a director at the time of her visit. City manager Donald J. Waring cuts the ribbon while members of the Samuel and David Rudman families, owners of the company, look on.

Another ribbon-cutting ceremony made news on February 10, 1960. City council chairman Gerald Robertson, second from the right, is accompanied, from left to right, by the following: F.W. Allingham, an IGA supply depot manager; store owner Louis Leakos; and Royce Banton, an IGA sales serviceman. The popular grocery was later sold to the Paradis family.

Brewer pulled out all the stops during the nation's bicentennial observance in 1976, even publishing a pictorial history edited by James B. Vickery. Contained in the book is this picture of businessman Robert Hall and his wife, Hazel. They are dressed in authentic Revolutionary War-era costumes while dancing the grand march at the Way Back Ball.

More than 300 friends and family members honored Duncan MacDonald at a 1968 testimonial held at the Brewer Auditorium. The 78-year-old city sports promoter was honored for his interest in harnessing racing and boxing in Maine. "Dunc" MacDonald was photographed with his granddaughter, Danielle Georgia, great-grandson, Michael Campbell, daughter Mrs. Emil Georgia (left), and granddaughter Mrs. Frank O'Toole.

Motorists driving along South Main Street were surprised in 1966 after mayor Barrington "Barry" Ivers, right, had this billboard erected spoofing a rash of UFO sightings throughout Maine as well as Brewer's eagerness to attract new business. The *Bangor Daily News* quipped, "So far, none has accepted but the invitation still stands."

ACKNOWLEDGMENTS

With kindness and generosity, many people and organizations helped make this book a reality. Most are located in Brewer, although a few are based outside the city's boundaries. At times, when I doubted the quality of my own work, they came through with words of encouragement. And when this Bangor native often grew red with embarrassment at his ignorance of certain aspects of Brewer's history, they smiled and walked me through its rich and colorful past. With the ever-present risk of omitting some individual or group that extended a helping hand, following is a list of those who shared their photographic collections, scrapbooks, and most exciting of all, their wisdom and knowledge.

Mildred N. Thayer invited me into her home and loaned images from her father, J. Craig Thayer's, collection; Elise Adams, library director of the Brewer Public Library and assistant library director Fran Payson shared their photographic archives and other historical material, including rare Chamberlain family pictures; Brian Higgins, president of the Brewer Historical Society, loaned many pictures from the society's collection and accompanied me on a tour of Chamberlain family landmarks; Brewer city clerk Archie Verow shared photographs of the Eastern Fine Paper Inc. and other treasures; Sue Wennrich, head reference librarian of the Bangor Public Library, and her staff let me examine the James Vickery photograph collection and other material; Paul E. Tower offered pictures and memories; Charles Campo and Jill Marston of the Bangor Daily News library staff offered assistance. Thanks also to Bangor bookseller Marc Berlin and his staff members, Gig Weeks and Ardeana Hamlin; Margo F. Cobb; Earle G. Shettleworth Jr. of the Maine Historic Preservation Commission; Rick Marston and his staff of Mail Boxes Etc.; Henry Wiswell; Brian Swartz; Jack and Muriel LaFountain; Pierre Dumont of *Paper Talks* magazine; Cecile, Phil, Jim, and Stella Morrill; Kalil and Eleanor Ayoob; Phil Joyce; Chris Downs; Stan and Eleanor Israel; the Maine Folklife Center; and last, but certainly not least, Marjorie Marsh Quigg.

Recommended reading:

Brewer, Orrington, Holden, Eddington: History & Families, history by Mildred N. Thayer and families by Mrs. Edward W. Ames.
A Pictorial History of Brewer, Maine, by James B. Vickery.
The City of Brewer, Maine, Centennial, 1889–1989, edited by James B. Vickery and Brian Swartz.
Steamboat Lore of the Penobscot, by John M. Richardson.
Sailing Days on the Penobscot, by George W. Wasson.
The Chamberlains of Brewer, by Diana Halderman Loski.

www.ingramcontent.com/pod-product-compliance
Lightning Source LLC
Chambersburg PA
CBHW080851100426
42812CB00007B/1988